WHY DOES MY BODY SMELL?

+ and other questions about hygiene +

Angela Royston

H **www.heinemann.co.uk/library**
Visit our website to find out more information about **Heinemann Library** books.

To order:
☎ Phone 44 (0) 1865 888066
🖹 Send a fax to 44 (0) 1865 314091
🖥 Visit the Heinemann Bookshop at www.heinemann.co.uk/library to browse our
catalogue and order online.

First published in Great Britain by Heinemann Library, Halley Court, Jordan Hill, Oxford
OX2 8EJ, a division of Reed Educational and Professional Publishing Ltd. Heinemann is a
registered trademark of Reed Educational & Professional Publishing Limited.

OXFORD MELBOURNE AUCKLAND JOHANNESBURG BLANTYRE
GABORONE IBADAN PORTSMOUTH NH (USA) CHICAGO

© Reed Educational and Professional Publishing Ltd 2002
The moral right of the proprietor has been asserted.

Designed by Joanna Sapwell and StoryBooks
Illustrations by Nick Hawken
Originated by Ambassador Litho Ltd
Printed in China by South China Printing Company

ISBN 0 431 11077 8
06 05 04 03 02
10 9 8 7 6 5 4 3 2 1

British Library Cataloguing in Publication Data
    Royston, Angela
    Why does my body smell?.– (Body matters)
    1. Body odour – Juvenile literature 2.
    I.Title
    612.7'92

Acknowledgements
The Publishers would like to thank the following for permission to reproduce photographs:
Action Plus: 7; Gareth Boden: 5, 6, 8, 10, 14, 15, 16, 17, 19, 22, 25, 26; Powerstock Zefa: 20; Science Photo
Library: 4, 9, 13, 18, 23, 24, 27, 28; Trevor Clifford: 12; Willibie Animal Photography: 21.

Cover photograph reproduced with permission of Gareth Boden.

Our thanks to Anne Long for her help in the preparation of this book.

Every effort has been made to contact copyright holders of any material reproduced in this book. Any omissions
will be rectified in subsequent printings if notice is given to the Publisher.

CONTENTS

Words printed in **bold letters like these** are explained in the Glossary.

WHY IS DIRT BAD FOR MY BODY?

Dirt contains millions of **germs**, some of which can make you ill in different ways. Germs are tiny forms of life that are too small to see except through a powerful microscope. They include **bacteria**, **viruses** and some kinds of **fungi**.

Bacteria and viruses

Bacteria are very small but they can multiply very fast. They breed fastest of all in warm, damp places, such as in your throat and lungs. Most bacteria that live inside your body and on your skin are harmless, but some can make you ill. Dirt often contains those kinds of bacteria. Viruses are even smaller than bacteria. More than 10,000 viruses could fit into the space of the smallest **bacterium**. Different kinds of virus cause different illnesses.

Bacteria are so small they have to be magnified at least 1000 times before you can see them. This kind of bacteria causes sore throats.

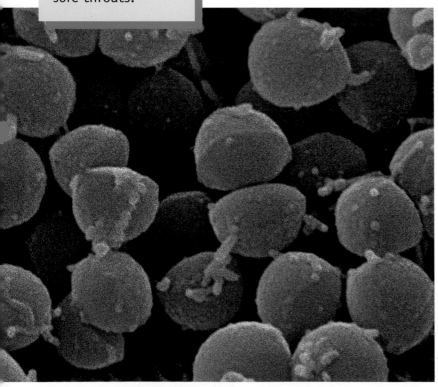

Fungi

There are many kinds of fungi and most of them do not make you ill. Field mushrooms and yeast are two kinds of fungi that are good to eat. But some fungi, such as those that cause athlete's foot, attack the body.

SOME ILLNESSES CAUSED BY GERMS

- bacteria: gum disease, stomach upsets, chest infection, conjunctivitis
- viruses: colds, warts, chickenpox, measles, polio
- fungi: athlete's foot, ringworm.

Protecting yourself against dirt

Your skin protects most of your body from dirt and germs. Germs cannot get through your skin unless it is cut or scratched. Most get inside your body through your nose or mouth, so it is important to wash dirt and germs off your skin, particularly your hands, before they spread to your nose or mouth.

This boy is licking ice cream off his fingers. If his fingers are dirty, germs from his skin will get inside his mouth and into his stomach.

WHY DO MY FEET SMELL?

Feet become smelly when they sweat and the sweat cannot escape into the air. Instead it soaks through your socks and into your trainers. The sweat in your trainers becomes stale and smells. When you wear the trainers again and your feet become hot and sweaty, the smell spreads to your socks and feet. Bare feet never become smelly from sweating.

This girl likes to wear trainers all day, but they make her feet smell.

Sweat

Your feet are not the only part of you that sweats. Your body makes between half and one litre of salty sweat a day. It oozes out all over your skin and you are not usually aware of it. Your body takes in and loses water every day. Sweating is just one of the ways that it loses water. When you are very hot, however, your body makes extra sweat which makes you feel damp and sticky. As the extra sweat **evaporates**, it helps to cool you down. It makes your skin cooler, but it leaves behind a thin layer of salt.

Bacteria

Pure sweat does not usually smell. It smells when bacteria live and breed in it, such as inside your trainers, between your toes and under your arms. Bacteria live on the salts and other substances contained in the sweat.

MOST SWEAT

The sweatiest parts of the body are the soles of the feet, the palms of the hand and the forehead. Sweat can also collect in your armpits.

Exercise makes you hot. The hotter you get the more you sweat.

Reducing the smell

The best way to stop sweat smelling is to use soap and water to wash away the stale sweat before bacteria can breed in it. Having a shower or bath every day washes your whole body and stops stale sweat from building up. If you cannot wash your whole body, you should wash the sweatiest parts, particularly your feet.

Showering washes away stale sweat and dirt and keeps you smelling clean and fresh.

Clean clothes

Sweat that gathers in socks and other clothes can also become smelly, so change your clothes regularly. If your feet are sweaty you will probably need to wear clean socks every day. If your trainers are very smelly, it may be possible to wash them too. If your trainers cannot be washed, you can buy special insoles (loose pads that fit inside your shoes) that help to kill the smell.

Deodorants

Deodorants are a good way of stopping sweat smelling. They contain chemicals that stop the **bacteria** breeding, and they usually contain a perfume that makes your skin smell fresh. Most deodorants are made for using on your armpits but some are made for the feet. Make sure you wash your skin before you apply the deodorant.

Antiperspirants

Many deodorants also contain an **antiperspirant** which stops the skin from sweating. But the skin needs to sweat, so, if you use an antiperspirant, make sure that you wash it off before you go to bed. Then your skin can sweat normally again.

This is what skin covered with sweat droplets looks like under a microscope. It contains many sweat glands. They pump salty water out of the body onto the skin.

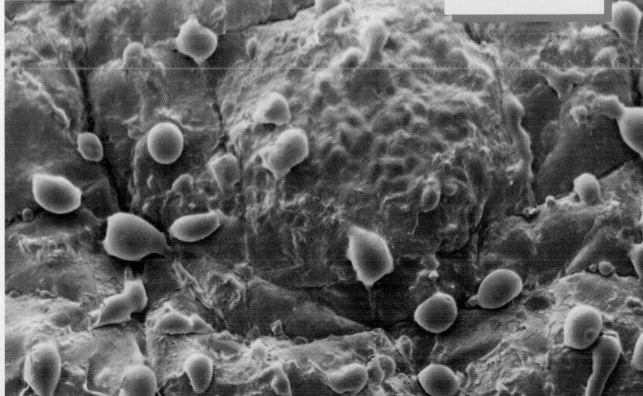

WHY DO I NEED TO BRUSH MY TEETH?

You need to brush your teeth to clean away tiny bits of food and **bacteria** that cling to your teeth. When you brush your teeth, brush from the gums to the tip of the teeth. Remember to brush the backs as well as the fronts. Then brush the tops of the large, flat molar teeth at the back of your mouth.

Teeth under attack

When you eat, tiny pieces of food dissolve in your **saliva** and cling around and between your teeth. Bacteria live and breed in the saliva. As bacteria feed on the bits of food, especially on sweet, sugary food, they produce a strong **acid**. The acid attacks the **enamel** that covers your teeth. Enamel is the hardest substance in your body, but it is not strong enough to resist the acid. The acid can make a hole, called a cavity, in the enamel. Then it attacks the softer **dentine** below.

Toothpaste contains special chemicals that help to remove food, saliva and bacteria from the surface of your teeth. It also leaves a fresh, clean taste in your mouth.

Toothache

If a cavity in a tooth is not filled by a dentist, it grows, until it attacks the pulp in the centre of the tooth. Then the tooth will begin to hurt very much.

Protecting your teeth

It is important to look after your teeth. The first set of teeth, the milk teeth, fall out between the ages of about five and twelve, but the adult teeth that grow to replace them have to last your whole life. You can protect your teeth by cleaning them regularly, using floss and visiting your dentist to have your teeth checked twice a year.

The inside of a tooth. Underneath the layer of hard enamel is dentine, which is as hard as bone. In the middle is a soft pulp.

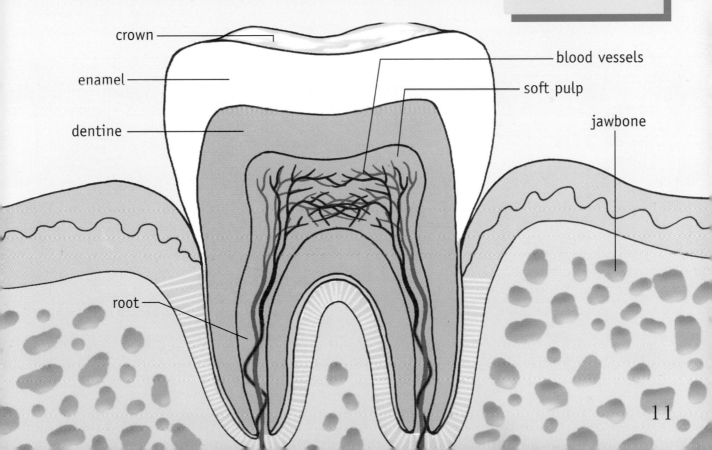

crown

enamel

dentine

blood vessels

soft pulp

jawbone

root

Cleaning your teeth

The best way to protect your teeth is to clean them regularly. You must certainly clean them every morning and in the evening before you go to bed. It also helps to clean them after eating or drinking anything sweet. If you cannot clean your teeth after eating, then a drink of water helps to wash away bits of leftover food and **bacteria** from your mouth.

This boy has sucked a disclosing tablet. It shows how much plaque he has by staining it blue. Now he has to clean his teeth well to brush away the plaque.

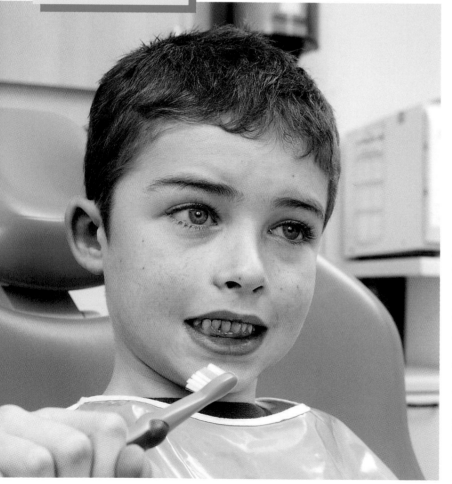

Dental floss

Plaque is a smelly paste that can build up around your teeth and under the edge of your gums. It consists of saliva and bacteria. It is difficult to remove all the plaque with a toothbrush. Dental floss is a thin string that you pull between your teeth and under the edge of your gums to remove any plaque that has built up there.

Dental check-ups

Dentists help to keep your teeth and mouth healthy. The dentist checks your gums and teeth. If a tooth has started to decay he or she will fill it with special chemicals to stop the hole getting any bigger. The dentist may coat your teeth with a layer of fluoride to protect them against decay.

WHAT IS IN TOOTHPASTE?

Toothpaste is a mixture of glycerol, a thick liquid, and:
- very fine chalk that scrubs your teeth
- a soapy substance that helps to remove dirt
- oil such as peppermint oil as a flavour
- a sweetener that contains no sugar.

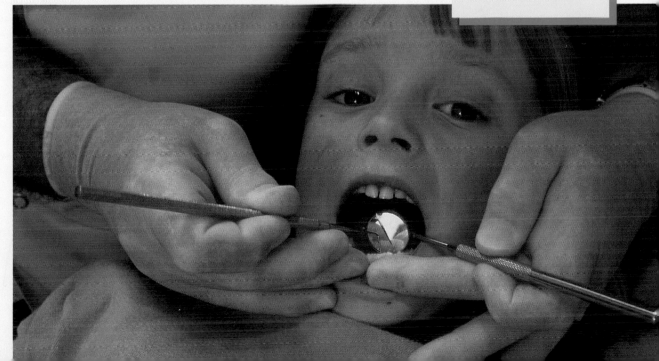

A dentist is using a small mirror and a metal probe to examine all around this child's teeth.

HOW DO GERMS SPREAD?

Illnesses that are passed from one person to another are said to be **infectious**. Some **germs** get inside the body when you breathe in air. Other germs spread to your body because you touch them without realising it. For example, if someone has a stomach upset they may have germs in their mouth or on their hands. If you drink from the same mug or can as them, the germs can spread from their mouth onto the mug and then into your mouth.

If you have a cold, always cover your mouth when you cough or sneeze so that you are less likely to pass on your germs.

Germs in the air

You cannot help breathing in germs – they are in the air all around you. With many illnesses, people breathe out germs with the stale air from their lungs. The germs float through the air and may be breathed in by other people, particularly people who are nearby. Colds, chickenpox and measles are caught in this way. When someone coughs or sneezes, millions of extra germs are launched into the air.

By direct contact

Some illnesses are **contagious**. This means you have to touch the germs to catch them. Conjunctivitis, for example, makes your eyes red and swollen. The germs that cause it have to touch your eyes. This is most likely to happen if you touch the germs without knowing it and then rub your eyes. Or you may come into contact with the germs in a swimming pool. If one of your friends has conjunctivitis, do not use their towel to dry your face because you will probably rub some of their germs into your eyes.

Always use your own towel to dry yourself. That way you are less likely to pick up other people's germs or pass on your own germs.

15

WHY SHOULD I WASH MY HANDS?

Your fingers and hands pick up germs easily because you touch things all the time. Washing your hands with soap and hot water cleans away the germs.

The best way to stop **germs** getting into your mouth is to wash your hands before you eat, after using the toilet and after handling pets.

Germs rub off onto your hands and fingers when you touch something that has germs on it. You cannot see them, but they can easily spread into your mouth when you touch your face. And if you eat something with your fingers, germs can rub off onto the food and pass into your mouth and stomach. Always wash your hands before you eat.

Be careful what you eat

Some food may contain a lot of germs. Fresh fruit and vegetables may have germs on the outside. Always peel or wash fruit and vegetables before you eat them. Be careful about eating food that has not been covered or wrapped. Flies like to settle on rubbish and on animal droppings, which are full of germs. Some of the germs rub off onto their bodies. If they then land on a cake, for example, that has been left uncovered, they will leave germs on the cake.

This girl is hungry but she cannot wash her hands. Instead she is making sure that her fingers do not touch the bar she is eating.

Fighting back

You do not have to protect yourself from every single germ, because your body is very good at fighting them. **Saliva** is slightly antiseptic which means that it can kill some of the germs. Although you may swallow the rest, strong **acid** in your stomach will kill them. But, if there are very many germs, they may multiply faster than your body can kill them and so make you sick.

Germs in the toilet

There are many germs in and around the toilet. They come from faeces – the solid waste that you and other people expel into the toilet. Many **bacteria** live naturally in the large intestine. They help to break down waste food and will not harm you while they remain there. When solid waste leaves your body, however, many of these bacteria pass out with it. Many spread onto your hands, so make sure you wash your hands after you have been to the toilet. If you do not, they may get into your mouth and make you ill.

Worms

Sometimes pinworms, or threadworms as they are often called, get inside your intestines and live and breed there. Pinworms are parasites. This means that they feed off your body.

This is a magnified photo of a pinworm. They make your skin itch, particularly at night.

Pinworms are harmless but they make your anus itchy and sore. They usually get inside your body as unhatched eggs which stick to your fingers and under your fingernails. The eggs are too small to see but pass into your mouth.

Worms can be cured by taking special medicine. The best way to avoid catching them, however, is to wash your hands after using the toilet and before eating.

Washing your hands after using the toilet will protect you against bacteria and from catching pinworms.

DON'T BE A SUCKER

Don't put pens, pencils, your thumb or anything else in your mouth. You don't know what germs, dirt or even eggs may be clinging to them!

Pets

Pets have many **germs** particularly in their mouths and in their droppings. It is nice to stroke, pick up and cuddle pets, but don't let their germs spread to you. The best way to prevent this happening is to wash your hands after handling animals and after cleaning out their cages.

Pets carry germs on their feet, in their fur and in their mouth. Wash your hands after handling a pet so that you do not catch their germs.

How animals spread germs

Animals often snuffle in rubbish and sniff each other's droppings. Don't let dogs lick your face. The **acid** in their stomachs is stronger than ours so germs around their mouths do not harm them, but the same germs can make us ill. Feathers and fur trap dirt, dust from the animal's own skin and germs. Although cats are well known for cleaning themselves, their fur is full of germs. You can help to keep your pet's fur clean by brushing and combing it, but don't forget to wash your hands afterwards.

Cleaning out their homes

Small pets such as rabbits, guinea pigs, hamsters and gerbils are usually kept in hutches or cages and these have to be cleaned regularly. You might give them fresh bedding material, but most of all you need to throw away old food, droppings and other debris from the floor of the hutch or cage. Cleaning washes away germs that can make your pet ill and stops the cage from smelling. Fish tanks and bowls also need to be cleaned regularly to keep the fish that live in them healthy.

This boy is cleaning out his rabbit's hutch. This will make it more comfortable for the rabbits and healthier for him and for them.

DO ONLY ATHLETES GET ATHLETE'S FOOT?

Athlete's foot usually starts as dry, itchy skin between the toes. Check your feet regularly and always dry them carefully.

Athlete's foot is caused by a **fungus** that usually grows between the toes and on the soles of the feet. It makes the skin itchy and flaky. Everyone who shares a bathroom or walks in bare feet will come into contact with the fungus, but some people catch it more easily than others. The fungus grows well in hot, moist places, such as an athlete's feet which are often hot and sweaty.

Avoiding athlete's foot

Try not to let your feet spend too long in sweaty socks and shoes. Wash carefully between the toes and dry your feet thoroughly on your own towel. If you use other people's towels you may catch the disease from them. Rubbing talcum powder between the toes helps to make sure they are completely dry.

This person is suffering from ringworm. The disease is caused by a fungus and has nothing to do with worms of any kind.

Treating athlete's foot

Washing and drying your feet carefully may be enough to get rid of the fungus. But, if not, you can get a special cream from the chemist that will soon cure it.

Ringworm

Ringworm is the name given to a skin condition caused by a fungus. Ringworm begins as a small red patch that spreads out. The skin in the middle of the patch heals, leaving a scaly ring which is often itchy. You can get ringworm on most parts of your skin but it is most common on the hands, arms, neck, scalp and chest. Ringworm is very **infectious** but is easy to cure by using a special cream.

HOW DO YOU CATCH VERRUCAS?

A verruca is a wart that forms on the sole of your foot. It is sometimes called a plantar wart. It is caused by a **virus** that gets into the top layer of skin through a crack, scratch or scrape. Verrucas are very **infectious** and spread easily, not only to other people but to another part of your foot. You catch them by walking on the virus in bare feet. If a verruca is not treated, it can become painful to walk on.

A wart is a bump in the skin. Warts are not very infectious and often disappear as unexpectedly as they appear.

Warts

Like verrucas, warts are caused by a virus in the top layer of your skin. Each wart contains millions of virus cells. Some of these cells have to get into your skin to infect you. The virus may stay in the skin for months before it develops into one or more warts. The warts appear as small bumps on the skin, usually on the hands or face. They are not very infectious and usually go away on their own, although it may take some time.

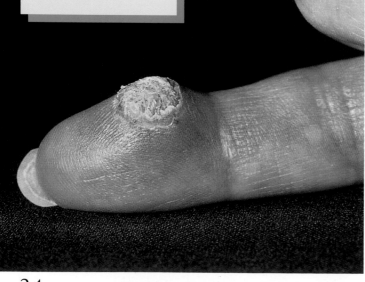

24

HOW TO AVOID SPREADING VERRUCAS:

- don't wear other people's shoes
- shower before and after swimming
- don't use other people's towels
- keep your verrucas under a watertight covering when you swim.

Verrucas affect the soles of your feet. You are most likely to catch them when you walk in bare feet or use a towel that has the virus on it.

Treating warts and verrucas

Chemists sell different ointments (creams) for warts and verrucas. Many ointments kill the skin around the verruca until the verruca falls away. If a verruca refuses to go away, a doctor can freeze it off or remove it with a laser.

HOW DO YOU GET NITS?

Nits are the empty eggs of head lice. You catch them when a head louse crawls into your hair and lays its eggs. Head lice feed by biting your scalp and sucking the blood. They can make your scalp incredibly itchy and this is the most common sign that you are infected. Head lice move fast and pass very easily from one head to another. If one person in a family is infected, everyone in the family is probably infected too.

Head lice

Head lice can crawl from one person's hair to another, even if their heads only touch for a moment.

Each louse lays many tiny eggs, which it sticks to a hair about a centimetre from the scalp. The new, young lice hatch about a week later, but the empty shell, or nit, remains glued to the hair. The young lice feed on your blood

and grow quickly. They start to lay their own eggs after about ten days, so the number of head lice in your hair increases rapidly.

Having head lice is not a sign that you have dirty hair. Head lice like to lay their eggs on clean hair.

Getting rid of head lice

You cannot wash head lice out of your hair with ordinary shampoo. You have to use a special shampoo or other treatment that kills the lice instead. A nit comb has teeth that are very close together. You should use it after treating your hair to comb out the dead lice. Lice spread so easily you cannot avoid them! The best way to stop them spreading is for everyone in your class at school and in your family to treat their hair for lice on the same night.

WHY DO I HAVE REGULAR MEDICAL CHECK-UPS?

You need to have a check-up from time to time to make sure that you are generally healthy. A doctor or nurse will measure your height and weight to make sure that you are growing well. Your eyes and ears will be tested to check that they are working properly.

This boy is being measured as part of a medical check-up.

Sight test

When your eyesight is tested you have to read large and small letters from a distance. People who are short-sighted cannot see distant things clearly. Long-sighted people find it difficult to read print in books or on labels. For people with astigmatism, everything may appear slightly blurred. All of these conditions can be corrected with glasses.

Hearing test

If the tubes inside your ears are blocked, you may have trouble hearing until the tubes are unblocked. Some people need a hearing aid to help them hear better.

BODY MAP

Check your hair for lice with a nit comb regularly

Regular medical check-ups will test your eyes and ears

Clean your teeth twice a day and visit the dentist every six months

Cover your mouth when you cough or sneeze

Wash your hands before eating, after using the toilet and after handling animals

Wash under your arms and other sweaty parts of the body every day

Check your feet regularly for verrucas and athlete's foot

Wash and dry your feet thoroughly

GLOSSARY

acid   liquid with a sour, bitter taste

antiperspirant   substance applied to the body to stop it sweating

bacteria   tiny living things. Some kinds of bacteria are germs that cause disease.

bacterium   single bacteria

contagious   when germs are passed from one person to another, by touching the germs themselves

dentine   part of a tooth below the enamel

deodorant   substance that stops sweat from smelling unpleasant

enamel   very hard substance that covers your teeth

evaporate   turn from water into tiny droplets in the air

fungi   living things that are like plants in many ways but have no green leaves

fungus   one kind of fungi

germs   microscopic forms of life that can make you ill

infectious   when germs that cause illness can be passed from one person to another

plaque sticky coat containing bacteria that builds up on teeth after eating

saliva fluid produced in the mouth which helps in the digestive process

virus kind of germ that is even smaller than all kinds of bacteria

FURTHER READING

Body works: The Senses, Paul Bennett, 1998, Belitha Press

Health matters: Hygiene and your health, Jillian Powell, 2002, Hodder Wayland

How our bodies work: Feel and Touch, Taste and Smell, Carol Ballard, 2001, Hodder Wayland

Look at your body: Brain and Nerves, S Parker, 2001, Franklin Watts

What about health? Hygiene, Cath Senker, 2001, Hodder Wayland

INDEX

Titles in the *Body Matters* series include:

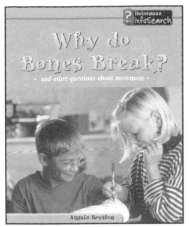

Hardback   0431 11075 1

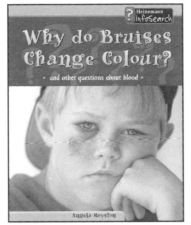

Hardback   0431 11073 5

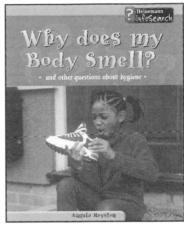

Hardback   0431 11077 8

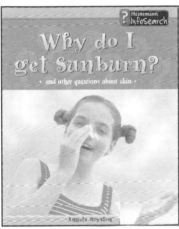

Hardback   0431 11078 6

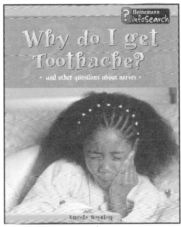

Hardback   0431 11076 X

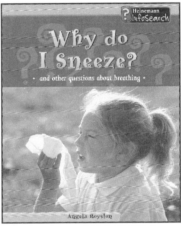

Hardback   0431 11070 0

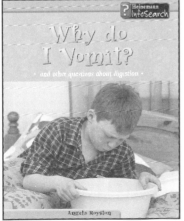

Hardback   0431 11072 7

Hardback   0431 11071 9

Find out about the other titles in this series on our website www.heinemann.co.uk/library